Seiyu Kiriyama, Founder of Agon Shu Buddhist Association

The *Heart Sutra* Meditation

by
Seiyu Kiriyama
Founder of Agon Shu Buddhist Association

HIRAKAWA SHUPPAN INC.

Copyright ©2002 by Seiyu Kiriyama
All rights reserved. No part of this publication may be reproduced without prior permission in writing from the publisher.

First published in 2002 by
HIRAKAWA SHUPPAN INC.
Mita 3-4-8, Minato-ku, Tokyo 108-0073, Japan

English version produced with cooperation of
Rande Brown and Fukiko Kai
Designed by Atsushi Sato
Printed and bound in Japan by TOPPAN Printing Co.,Ltd.
Paper supplied by NAKASHO, Inc.

Contents

Reciting the *Heart Sutra*.........07

The *Heart Sutra*
(*Bussetsu Maka Hannyaharamita Shingyo*)...08

An Invitation to the *Heart Sutra* Meditation.........13

What Is the "*Heart Sutra*"?...14
What Is the "*Heart Sutra* Meditation"?...14
Preparing to Meditate...15
Seed-Syllables (*Shuji*), Mantras (*Shingon*),
and Mudras (*Ingei*)...16
  What Are "Seed-Syllables"?...16
  What Are "Mantras"?...16
  What Are "Mudras"?...17
Avalokiteshvara Bodhisattva
(Kanjizai Bosatsu)...17
  Seed-Syllable...17
  Mantra...17
  Mudra...18
Prajnaparamita Bodhisattva
(Hannyaharamita Bosatsu)...18
  Seed-Syllable...18
  Mantra...18
  Mudra...19

A Guide to Meditation...21

Introduction...24
    Placing Palms Together (*Gassho*)...24
    Lighting Incense...24
How to Sit...24
    The Lotus Position (*Kekkafuza*)...24
    The Half-Lotus Position (*Hankafuza*)...25
    The "Chair" Sitting Position...25
    The Japanese (*Yamato*) Sitting Position...26
Getting Your Body Ready...26
Breathing Exercises...27
    Long Inhalation (*Chonyusoku*)...27
    Long Exhalation (*Choshussoku*)...28
    Combined Long Inhalation and Exhalation
      (*Choshutsunyusoku*)...28
Breath-Counting (*Susokukan*)...29

How to Practice the *Heart Sutra* Meditation...31

Placing Palms Together (*Gassho*)...32
Obeisance (*Raihai*)...32
Verse of Devotion Prior to Chanting Sutra
  (*Kaikyoge*)...32
Reciting the *Heart Sutra*
  (*Hannya Shingyo Dokuju*)...32
Pledges (*Seigan*)...33
Visualization of Vast Emptiness (*Daikokukan*)...34
Visualization of Lunar Disc (*Gachirinkan*)...35

The Syllable "*Sa*" 社 Appears in the Middle
of the Lunar Disc...36
The Syllable "*Sa*" 社 Changes into
Avalokiteshvara...37
The Syllable "*Ja*" 煮 Appears in the Middle
of the Lunar Disc...38
The Syllable "*Ja*" 煮 Changes into
Prajnaparamita...39
Meditation on Dependent Co-arising, Transformation,
and Water (*Engi Ruten Suisokan*)...40
Meditation on Three Circles within a Triangle
(*Sankaku Daienkukan*)...42
Triangular Wisdom Mudra (*Sankaku Chiin*)...44
Bodhisattva of Wish-fulfilling Radiance
(Shonyoiko Bosatsu)...45
Visualization of Avalokiteshvara Emitting Light Rays
(Kanjizai Bosatsu *Daibukkokan*)...46
Conclusion...47

Reciting the *Heart Sutra*

The *Heart Sutra*
(*Bussetsu Maka Hannyaharamita Shingyo*)

Translated by the monk Hsuan-tsang (Xuanzang, 600–664) of the T'ang Dynasty from Sanskrit into Chinese.

Japanese Reading

Kanjizai Bosatsu
Gyo Jin Hannya Haramita Ji
Shoken Go'un Kai Ku
Do Issai Kuyaku
Sharishi
Shiki Fu I Ku
Ku Fu I Shiki
Shiki Soku Ze Ku
Ku Soku Ze Shiki
Ju So Gyo Shiki Yaku Bu Nyoze
Sharishi
Ze Shoho Kuso
Fusho Fumetsu
Fuku Fujo
Fuzo Fugen
Ze Ko Ku Chu
Mu Shiki
Mu Ju So Gyo Shiki
Mu Gen Ni Bi Zetsu Shin Ni
Mu Shiki Sho Ko Mi Soku Ho

Mu Genkai
Naishi Mu Ishikikai
Mu Mumyo
Yaku Mu Mumyo Jin
Naishi Mu Roshi
Yaku Mu Roshi Jin
Mu Ku Ju Metsu Do
Mu Chi Yaku Mu Toku
I Mu Shotoku Ko
Bodaisatta
E Hannya Haramita Ko
Shin Mu Keige
Mu Keige Ko
Mu U Kufu
Onri Issai Tendo Muso
Kugyo Nehan
Sanze Shobutsu
E Hannya Haramita Ko
Toku Anokutara Sanmyaku Sanbodai
Ko Chi Hannya Haramita
Ze Dai Jinshu
Ze Dai Myoshu
Ze Mujoshu
Ze Mu Todoshu
No Jo Issai Ku
Shinjitsu Fu Ko Ko
Setsu Hannya Haramita Shu

Soku Setsu Shu Watsu
Gyatei
Gyatei
Haragyatei
Harasogyatei
Boji Sowaka

Hannya Shingyo

Interpretative Translation

The Bodhisattva Avalokiteshvara entered the deep practice of wisdom to save the world from suffering. At the culmination of his practice he understood that all the five aggregates (all things) are empty, thereby attaining liberation from all suffering.

"Listen, Shariputra. I will explain this teaching. Be flexible, don't be captivated by forms, which can change. Even if something has assumed a form because of conditions, different conditions may cause it to disappear.

"Even if something has no form, do not assume that it does not exist. Different conditions may cause it to appear.

"Think about water. If the water is subjected to conditions conducive to heat, it changes into hot water and into vapor, and blends with the sky. If it is then chilled, it becomes water again and falls to earth as rain. If it is subjected to conditions conducive to freezing, it turns into snow and ice. The intrinsic nature of water doesn't change; only the conditions to which it is subjected change, resulting in different forms.

"Everything in the world is the same. Whether things have forms or not depends entirely on direct causes and indirect conditions.

"It is the same with the functions of the human mind, feelings, thoughts, actions, and consciousness. All follow this principle. People experience grief, sadness, and joy. However, this does not mean that people have fixed feelings of grief, sadness, and joy in their minds.

"In keeping with the principle of direct causes and indirect conditions, indirect conditions arise in response to direct causes, making forms appear temporarily. This is called the principle of emptiness.

"Listen, Shariputra. The original nature of everything is emptiness, and everything is transformed into various forms because of different conditions. However, its original nature does not change. It neither arises nor is extinguished. There is neither purity nor defilement, neither increase nor decrease. What exists is only the changes.

"Listen, Shariputra. If you understand this principle and apply it to this world, then things that have form are the same as things that do not have form. There are no feelings, thoughts, mental formations, or consciousness. No eye, ear, nose, tongue, body, or mind. Therefore, there is no form, sound, smell, taste, touch, or mind-object. There is no realm of vision, or realm of consciousness; no ignorance, therefore, no end to ignorance. There is no old age and no death, and no end to aging and death. You should know that there is no suffering, delusion, cessation, or path, and no wisdom and no attainment. Put such things out of your mind. If you understand this truth, all obstacles will leave your mind. If you are free from obstacles, you will not experience delusion, fear, or desires. You must understand the principle of emptiness. Freed from delusion, you can arrive at Nirvana.

"All the Buddhas of the past, present, and future rely on this understanding to attain the supreme wisdom of enlightenment.

"For this reason, we who seek the truth must know the Prajnaparamita mantra. It is the highest, most incomparable mantra—a mantra that gives relief from all suffering, a mantra of incalculable power, offering the truth of all truths. Because of its truth, it is never-changing, applying in all worlds and at all times."

This mantra says:
"Practice, keep practicing, and if you keep practicing,
You will eventually reach the other shore,
Where you will be free from suffering. Svaha!"

Reciting the *Heart Sutra*

An Invitation to the *Heart Sutra* Meditation

What Is the "*Heart Sutra*"?

The Buddhist scriptures consist of about 7,000 scrolls. Among them, there is a short sutra of only 262 characters which embodies the essence of the Buddhist teachings. It is known as the *Heart Sutra* and contains the materials necessary for attaining enlightenment. As such, it is chanted not only in most of the Buddhist sects of Japan, but also far and wide throughout Asia.

The *Heart Sutra* is known as the *Prajnaparamita Hridaya Sutra* in the original Sanskrit and *Hannyaharamita Shingyo* (its full name) or *Hannya Shingyo* (its short name) in Japanese. It is the ultimate guide to practices that lead to the highest wisdom and the core of the teachings on "the other shore," nirvana. Nirvana, which is liberation from the bonds of illusion and suffering, is the goal of the Buddha's teachings. Practicing wisdom is the way to reach the goal of nirvana.

In other words, the *Heart Sutra* shows the way to return to the practice of wisdom, which is the point from which the Buddha started. It is a meditation textbook to let practitioners attain the saintly enlightenment that comes from understanding emptiness.

What Is the "*Heart Sutra* Meditation"?

The "*Heart Sutra* Meditation" is a practical system that will allow anyone to meditate easily on the *Heart Sutra*. You will not be able to attain the enlightenment and the truth of emptiness just by chanting the *Heart Sutra* thousands and thousands of times. The only way is by saintly meditation on the *Heart Sutra* mandala.

First, the practitioner enters a state of deep concentration on the Bodhisattva Avalokiteshvara. Then the practitioner enters a deeper stage of meditation on the wisdom of the *Heart Sutra*. This means that you yourself can become the Bodhisattva Avalokiteshvara and gain true wisdom.

Practice, keep practicing, and if you keep practicing,
You will eventually reach the other shore,
Where you will be free from suffering. Svaha!

Preparing to Meditate

Here I will explain how you should get ready to meditate.

You don't need any special items in order to meditate.

I recommend that the room where you meditate should be quiet, not too large, and without distractions.

The room should be neat, and not too bright or too dark. In addition, the room temperature should be adjusted to be moderate, not too cold or too hot.

Hang the mandala on the wall in front of you, and offer incense and flowers.

Incense helps you to know how much time has passed.

I recommend that you always use it.

These are the basic preparations. Ideally, however, you should be mentally ready to practice meditation at any time, in any place, and under any conditions. You should meditate freely, without constraints, and in a relaxed manner. You won't be able to continue for a long time if you think of it as hard and difficult. Sit and enter meditation in the same light mood as if you were exercising along with a TV program.

Seed-Syllables (*Shuji*), Mantras (*Shingon*), and Mudras (*Ingei*)

Now I will explain three terms—seed-syllable, mantra, and mudra—that are associated with meditation on the *Heart Sutra*.

What Are "Seed-Syllables"?

"Seed-syllable" refers to a Sanskrit syllable that represents the power of Buddhas and Bodhisattvas. Just as the seeds of plants grow into roots, stems, leaves, flowers, and so on with the help of rain, dew, and sunlight, so too does a single syllable encapsulate the power of Buddhas and Bodhisattvas.

What Are "Mantras"?

"Mantra" refers to a word or phrase with profound meanings related to the pledges, virtues, and enlightenment of Buddhas and Bodhisattvas.

What Are "Mudras"?
"Mudra" is a sign or gesture made with the hands and fingers. Combinations of mudras express the inner heart of Buddhas and Bodhisattvas.

Avalokiteshvara Bodhisattva (Kanjizai Bosatsu)
The practice of Buddhism is intended to save people from the suffering of this world. Changing into 33 forms, Avalokiteshvara saves people from misfortune and gives them happiness.

Seed-Syllable
The seed-syllable of Avalokiteshvara is the syllable *"sa"* 𑖭, which represents inapprehensibility of the three truths, namely, that existence is void, that it has a provisional reality, and that there is a supreme truth. Avalokiteshvara uses these truths to awaken and enlighten everyone who is lost and deluded.

Mantra
On Bazaratarama Kiriku

Mudra
The Mudra of Avalokiteshvara

Clasp the palms together with the fingers on the outside; both index fingers are slightly bent to make an oval shape and both thumbs are placed together to resemble a lotus leaf.

Prajnaparamita Bodhisattva (Hannyaharamita Bosatsu)

This is a Buddha who represents the wisdom of *prajna*. She became a Buddha by gaining enlightenment through this wisdom, and gives birth to Buddhas. She is known as the mother of Buddhas.

Seed-Syllable
The seed-syllable of Prajnaparamita is the syllable *"ja"* ज. This syllable expresses the inapprehensibility of birth and argument.

Mantra
Great Heart Dharani of Wisdom
(*Hannya Daishin Darani*)
Tanyata Gyatei Gyatei Haragyatei
Harasogyatei Boji Sowaka

Basic Incantation of the Inexhaustible Treasury of

Wisdom (*Hannya Konpon Mujinzo Ju*)
Nobo Bagyabati
Harashaharamitaei On
Riiji Ishiri
Shurotabishaei Sowaka

Mantra of the Bodhisattva Prajnaparamita
(Hannyaharamita Bosatsu *Inmyo*)
On Ji Shirishurotabijaei Sowaka

Mudra
The mudra when reciting the second mantra is the "scripture stand" (*kyodai*) mudra, which represents the positioning of the Buddhist scriptures on a stand of honor, and you touch your heart with the mudra.

You then chant a mystical invocation, and imagine that all Buddhist scriptures emanate from this mudra and then enter your heart. You then should focus your thoughts so as to generate an endless number of sutras and completely understand all wise teachings.

The mudra when reciting the third mantra is the "scripture" (*bonkyo*) mudra. This mudra is formed by extending your left palm, covering it with your inverted right palm so that both palms are in contact, and touching your heart with the mudra. Then, if you chant this mantra three times, you will do away with the infinite sufferings due to your ignorance, and you will complete your practice of meditation, allowing you to gain supreme wisdom.

A Guide to Meditation

The *Heart Sutra* Meditation is a type of meditation based on the *Heart Sutra*. It is organized so that anyone can practice it anytime and anywhere. This guidebook comes with a DVD, and presents in a clear manner how to master the *Heart Sutra* Meditation.

Since the time of Buddha, adherents have followed practices intended to search out truth and cut off worldly desires. The *Heart Sutra* is a textbook that will help a truth-seeker to experience the saintly enlightenment that comes from understanding emptiness. You too can attempt to be transformed into a Avalokiteshvara Bodhisattva, so let's practice the mediation that lets you attain ultimate wisdom (*prajnaparamita*).

The length of a single meditation (from assuming a sitting position to leaving the position) should initially be about 15 minutes, and you should try to gradually lengthen the duration to 30 or 40 minutes.

In principle, mediation procedures should be carried out in a certain order. However, you have to practice repeatedly, training yourself until you master the proper way to sit, to breathe, and visualize. When you want to mediate for longer periods, pause the DVD on a still image.

You should breathe slowly and quietly during meditation.

It is more important to practice meditation for one sitting every day than to meditate for a long period.
Even if it is difficult at the beginning, it will gradually become enjoyable, and in the end you won't be able to spare one day without practicing meditation.

After you master it, you'll be able to mediate without the help of the DVD because you'll be able to visualize images all by yourself. So you should practice hard to reach this stage.
Meditation will not have noticeable effects immediately. However, you'll be surprised at the changes in yourself as you continue.

There is an ancient saying in the West:
"Only those who practice meditation have succeeded in achieving great things."

Introduction

The first step is to sit quietly and tranquilly. Relax and be comfortable. To do this, you should have a *"zafu"* cushion handy.

Placing Palms Together (*Gassho*)
To begin, join your palms together, as in prayer.

Lighting Incense
Light incense. I recommend using incense to let you know how much time has passed.

How to Sit

You can practice the *Heart Sutra* Meditation either sitting on the floor or sitting in a chair. The important thing is to be at ease and relaxed.

There are four sitting positions.

Stand facing your cushion and sit, after joining your palms together, as in prayer.

The Lotus Position (*Kekkafuza*)
Resting your buttocks on the cushion, extend your legs in front. Holding the big toe of your right foot with your right hand, raise your foot and place it on top of your left thigh so that your heel touches your belly.

Next, holding the big toe of your left foot with your

left hand, raise your foot and place it on top of your right thigh so that your heel touches your belly in the same way. With your legs intertwined, the soles of your feet should be facing the ceiling.

Another name for this position is the "tripod," because your body is supported at three points: your two knees and your coccyx (tailbone), forming an equilateral triangle. This is an extremely good position because it is stable and natural.

The Half-Lotus Position (*Hankafuza*)

The lotus position is the most stable position, but it is difficult for some beginners to intertwine their legs properly. The half-lotus position is suitable until you master a more advanced position. In the half-lotus position, you place the bottom of your right foot firmly against the inside of your left thigh and only place your left foot on top of your right thigh. If you feel pain, you can alternate between left and right foot.

The important thing about this position is that one knee will be unsupported and may be unstable. If this happens, just add one more cushion under your buttocks, which will raise your body. Then lean forward a bit so that your two knees touch the floor, and straighten your torso.

The "Chair" Sitting Position

The third way is to sit on a chair. If you use this position, you should loosen your belt and clothing. You should sit slightly forward on the edge of the chair with your legs slightly open and both feet firmly planted on the floor.

The Japanese (*Yamato*) Sitting Position
I recommend the Japanese sitting position for those people who cannot use the lotus or half-lotus position. This position means sitting on your heels in the traditional Japanese way of sitting on *tatami* mats. In this position, there should be a little space between your knees. Men should have a space of three fists between their knees, while women should have a space of two fists. Using the "*zafu*" cushion will make this position more stable.

Getting Your Body Ready
Massage your body. Then gently rotate your feet to loosen them up. Sway slowly forwards and backwards and from side to side eight times, and rotate your neck and shoulders to loosen the tension in your body.

Pull in your chin and incline your forehead slightly forward. At the same time, pull in your chest while thrusting your belly slightly forward, relax your shoulders, and assume a natural posture. Your back should be inclined slightly forward.

Close your eyes to a slit so that you can see only a little light and gaze at the tip of your nose. Close your anus tight and try to elevate it.

Next, open your mouth and exhale as much breath as possible from the bottom of your belly. Imagine that all impurities in your body are being expelled with your breath. Close your mouth after exhaling your breath. Then breathe in pure air through your nostrils.

Repeat this procedure three times. If you can do it rhythmically, with good coordination, once will be enough.

The important thing is not to overdo it. Don't relax too much and don't get too uptight. You should try to be as natural as possible.

Breathing Exercises

Breathing techniques always start by exhaling the breath. Press your upper and lower teeth lightly together and exhale your breath gently through the gaps between your teeth. After doing so, your first breath inhaled commences the count of the breathing exercise.

Long Inhalation (*Chonyusoku*)

Close your lips, placing the upper and lower teeth together. The tip of your tongue should touch the upper portion of your gums.

Now, start breathing in naturally and slowly through your nostrils.

After completing your inhalation, tighten your anus, and make the abdomen your center of gravity.

At the same time, exhale a little breath through your nostrils. If you don't do this, you will feel pressure all the way from your chest to your head and you might even hurt your body. Sometimes abdominal or deep breathing causes headaches or visceroptosis (downward displacement of the abdominal organs) because people don't know the technique above to prevent it.

Long Exhalation (*Choshussoku*)
Now I will explain long exhalation.

Exhale slowly through the gaps in your teeth while pressing your teeth lightly together. Focusing your strength in your lower abdomen to keep your center of gravity there, exhale quietly, keeping your strength in your lower abdomen until you complete exhaling.

Combined Long Inhalation and Exhalation (*Choshutsunyusoku*)
This is just one set of the long inhalation and exhalation techniques I have just described. It does not matter how long each combined inhalation and exhalation is; just breathe in and out as slowly and gently as you can.

Repeat it from three to five times.

Breath-Counting (*Susokukan*)

The combined long inhalation and exhalation technique has prepared you to undertake breath-counting.

This is a meditation technique that concentrates your mind on counting breaths and prevents you from being distracted.

Exhale so that you feel you are breathing from the pit of your stomach toward the sky. Pretend you are following the course taken by your exhalation with your mind's eye. Without vocalization, begin the first half of the Japanese word for the number "one"—HITO.... Then breathe in, and complete the second half of the word—TSU.

Count up to ten in Japanese in this manner. Then go back to the beginning—count one, and repeat this procedure many times. (1: *hitotsu*, 2: *futatsu*, 3: *mittsu*, 4: *yottsu*, 5: *itsutsu*, 6: *muttsu*, 7: *nanatsu*, 8: *yattsu*, 9: *kokonotsu*, 10: *to*.)

The important thing is not to have any gaps between inhalation and exhalation; it should feel smooth and egg-shaped, with each cycle of inhalation and exhalation like an egg. More specifically, you should begin breathing in before you have completed exhaling, and start breathing out before you have completed breathing in. This makes you feel natural and relaxed.

The most important thing about breath-counting is to properly coordinate breathing and counting. You retain a focus on the mind's eye by concentrating on counting and tracing the course taken by your exhalations.

Practice this breathing technique for a while. Once you feel ready and stable, we can go on to the next steps.

How to Practice
the *Heart Sutra* Meditation

Placing Palms Together (*Gassho*)
Place your two palms together in the prayer position.

Obeisance (*Raihai*)
Make a bow of reverence.

Verse of Devotion Prior to Chanting Sutra (*Kaikyoge*)
This is the verse of devotion recited before chanting a sutra.

Mujo Jin Jin Mimyo Ho
Hyakusenman Go Nan Sogu
Ga Kon Kenmon Toku Juji
Gan Ge Nyorai Shinjitsu Gi

Translated, it means: "Hard is it to find an unsurpassed, profound, and excellent teaching in countless eons. Now we have encountered and received it. May we understand the true principle taught by the Tathagata."

Reciting the *Heart Sutra* (*Hannya Shingyo Dokuju*)
Now recite the *Heart Sutra* either in a low voice or

voicelessly.

Pledges (*Seigan*)

Here are the pledges made by aspirants to Buddhahood. Following are the pledges you should make.

"I pledge sincerely to the World-Honored One Shakyamuni, the Bodhisattva and Mahasattva Avalokiteshvara, and the Bodhisattva and Mahasattva Prajnaparamita. From this stage, I will transform myself into Avalokiteshvara and will try to attain the supreme wisdom. From the bottom of my heart, I beseech your help in reaching this goal without hindrance."

Visualization of Vast Emptiness
(*Daikokukan*)

Now you will enter a realm of vast emptiness.

The mudra for this stage is called "Akasha." Extend both arms in a natural fashion, placing your hands on your knees with the index finger and thumb forming a circle.

Imagine yourself in an infinite emptiness, beyond the solar system and the Milky Way.

You are sitting in the center of this emptiness.

Visualization of Lunar Disc
(*Gachirinkan*)

Now you will practice the visualization of a lunar disc.

Sit, making the Akasha mudra on both knees.

Imagine a pure, white full moon hanging two meters before your eyes.

Close your eyes and slowly pull the moon into your chest.

You imagine the pure, white moon growing and becoming infinitely large.

Then you reduce the size of the infinitely large moon, bringing it back to its original size.

Then you open your eyes and return the moon to the sky.

The *Heart Sutra* Meditation

The Syllable "*Sa*" ཨ Appears in the Middle of the Lunar Disc

Place your two palms together in the prayer position.

You will see the syllable "*sa*" appear in the middle of the pure, white moon.
The syllable will be emitting golden rays.

The Syllable "*Sa*"ས Changes into Avalokiteshvara

Make the mudra of Avalokiteshvara.

The syllable "*sa*" that is emitting golden rays is transformed into Avalokiteshvara. The entire body of Avalokiteshvara will shine brightly.

The brightness will shine on you. Upon receiving the shining light of Avalokiteshvara, your body will begin to emit light. When your body emits light, you will be one and united with Avalokiteshvara.

The *Heart Sutra* Meditation

The Syllable "*Ja*" 🕉 Appears in the Middle of the Lunar Disc

Place your two palms together in the prayer position.

The syllable "*ja*" will appear in the middle of the pure, white moon.

It will be emitting bright golden rays.

The Syllable "*Ja*" 🐎 Changes into Prajnaparamita

Make the "scripture stand" (*kyodai*) mudra.

Rays of brilliant light will come from the box of Buddhist scriptures in the first left hand of the Bodhisattva. Your "scripture stand" mudra will also begin emitting light.

Enter a deep state of meditation.

Meditation on Dependent Co-arising, Transformation, and Water
(*Engi Ruten Suisokan*)

"Listen, Shariputra. Be flexible, don't be captivated by forms, which can change. Even if something has assumed a form because of conditions, different conditions may cause it to disappear.

"Even if something has no form, do not assume that it does not exist. Different conditions may cause it to appear.

"Think about water. If the water is subjected to conditions conducive to heat, it changes into hot water and into vapor, and blends with the sky. If it is then chilled, it becomes water again and falls to earth as rain. If it is subjected to conditions conducive to freezing, it turns into snow and ice. The intrinsic nature of water doesn't change; only the conditions to which it is subjected change, resulting in different forms.

"Everything in the world is the same. Whether things have forms or not depends entirely on direct causes and indirect conditions.

"It is the same with the functions of the human mind, feelings, thoughts, actions, and consciousness. All follow this principle. People experience grief, sadness, and joy. However, this does not mean that people have fixed feelings of grief, sadness, and joy in their minds.

"In keeping with the principle of direct causes and indirect conditions, indirect conditions arise in response to direct causes, making forms appear temporarily. This is called the principle of emptiness."

(Interpretative translation of the *Heart Sutra*)

You should meditate on the universe, human relationships, and everything else in keeping with this meditation on dependent co-arising, transformation, and water.

Meditation on Three Circles within a Triangle (*Sankaku Daienkukan*)

Make the Akasha mudra with your hands on both knees.

Imagine a huge triangle in the sky.
Imagine a large circle at each corner.
Divide your thoughts in three.

Put the things that have forms into the circle for forms. Think about things that have physical shapes. If it is hard to do this, think about the person you dislike most, and put that person in the circle for forms.

Next is the circle for words. If it is hard to think of words to put in it, think of words of hatred, and put those words in the circle.

Last is the circle for concepts. If it is hard to think of concepts to put in it, compress thoughts of hatred, and put them in the circle.

Separate all your thoughts and feelings into these three categories and put them in the right circles. Separate all your anger, grudges, and earthly desires into these three categories and put them in the right circles. Put yourself in a circle too.

Erase everything in the circles one by one so that all the circles become empty.

Lastly, erase yourself, so that you become an empty circle.

Erase everything, make it empty, and make a huge empty circle.

The *Heart Sutra* Meditation

Triangular Wisdom Mudra
(*Sankaku Chiin*)

Make the Akasha mudra.

Flames will appear in the big circle you have just made.

The big flames will then be transformed into the triangular wisdom mudra.

Our supreme wisdom will flame up in the shape of the mudra.

The big flame in the shape of the mudra will pervade vast emptiness.

Bodhisattva of Wish-fulfilling Radiance (Shonyoiko Bosatsu)

The mudra is called the "wish-fulfilling gem" (*nyoihoju*).

The Bodhisattva of Wish-fulfilling Radiance will appear in the vast emptiness. Our supreme wisdom becomes a wish-fulfilling gem that emits brilliant light.

There is a wish-fulfilling gem in our mudra. Gleaming brightly, it emits light into the vast emptiness.

Visualization of Avalokiteshvara Emitting Light Rays
(Kanjizai Bosatsu *Daibukkokan*)

Make the Avalokiteshvara mudra.

Avalokiteshvara emits bright rays.

Your body becomes the same as Avalokiteshvara and gleams brightly.

Conclusion

To conclude the meditation, you should free your heart from meditation.

Say clearly to yourself, "This ends my meditation. From now on, I will use my supreme wisdom to live in the world as Avalokiteshvara."

Release the mudra.

Place your hands together in prayer.

Sway your torso to the left and right four or five times.

Open your mouth and exhale three times.

Rub your hands together, cover your eyes, uncover them, open your eyes wide, and look slowly around.

Massage your legs, place your hands on the floor, and your heels firmly on the floor to stand up.

Place your hands together in prayer facing your cushion, and leave.

Be certain to make meditation a daily habit.

Prayer and Meditation

Prayer and meditation can make anyone a god or Buddha.

About the Author

Seiyu Kiriyama

Founder of Agon Shu Buddhist Association
Professor Emeritus, Peking University
Professor Emeritus, Beijing Foreign Studies University
Professor Emeritus, Zhongshan University
Professor Emeritus, National Buddhist Seminary of China (Buddhist College)
Professor Emeritus and Honorary Doctor of Philosophy, National University of Mongolia
Honorary Doctor of Philosophy, Mongolian Academy of Sciences
Visiting Professor and Honorary Dean, Nyingmapa Tibetan Buddhist College
Honorary Doctor of Journalism and Mass Communication, Thammasat University
Member of Board of Directors, University of San Francisco
Honorary SOAS Fellow, University of London
Honorary High Priest, Siam Nikaya Order of Sri Lankan Buddhism
Title of Highest Clerical Rank in Tibetan and Myanmarese Buddhism
Dharma lineage and full proficiency in the secret dharmas of Bhutanese Buddhism; conferred title of 'Ngawang Gyaltshen' (Protector of Buddhist Teachings Who Preaches Royal Sermons)
Director, International Qigong Research Center (Beijing)
Honorary Member, Dutch Treat Club (New York City)
Honorary Ninth *Dan*, Nihon Ki'in (Japan Go Association)
Honorary Vice Chairman, Zhongguo Weiqi Xiehui (Chinese Go Association)

Seiyu Kiriyama has written 70 books,
including *Agon Buddhism as the Source of Shamatha (Tranquility) and Vipashyana (Insight)* ; *The Varieties of Karma; 21st Century: The Age of Sophia; You Have Been Here Before: Reincarnation; The Wisdom of the Goma Fire Ceremony; The Marvel of Spiritual Transformation and Sacred Buddhist Fire Ceremony for World Peace 2001; Practicing Meditation for Reincarnation,* Parts I-III.

Agon Shu Office Addresses

Main Temple
Shakazan Daibodai-ji
Omine-cho, Yamashina-ku,
Kyoto, JAPAN

Kanto Main Office
Agon Shu Kanto Betsuin
4-14-15 Mita, Minato-ku, Tokyo
108-8318, JAPAN
Tel:81-3-3769-1931

Kansai Main Office
Agon Shu Kansai So-hombu
Jingumichi Agaru, Sanjodori,
Higashiyama-ku, Kyoto
605-0031, JAPAN
Tel:81-75-761-1141

Europe Branch Office
Agon Shu UK
First Floor, 31-33 Bondway,
London SW8 1SJ, England UK
Tel:44-20-7587-5179

Canada Branch Office-Toronto Office
Agon Shu Canada Buddhist Association
18 Wynford Drive, Suite 608 Toronto,
ON M3C 0K8 Canada
Tel:1-416-922-1272

Brazil Branch Office
Associação Budista Agon Shu
Rua Dr. Nogueira Martinş, 247
Saúde-São Paulo, BRAZIL
CEP:04143-020
Tel:55-11-3876-8812

Taiwan Main Dojo
Agon Shu Taiwan Honzan Dojo
1F., No.27-6, Sec 2,
Zhongshang N. Rd.,
Tamsui Dist., New Taipei City 251,
TAIWAN(ROC)
Tel:886-2-2808-4601

Taichung Taiwan Dojo
Agon Shu Taichu Dojo
Rm. B, 2F., No. 447, Sec. 3,
Wenxin Rd., Beitun Dist.,
Taichung City 406,
TAIWAN(ROC)
Tel:886-4-2298-3380

Kaohsiung Taiwan Dojo
Agon Shu Takao Dojo
Rm. 1, 13F., No. 80, Minzu 1st. Rd.,
Sanmin Dist., Kaohsiung City 807,
TAIWAN(ROC)
Tel:886-7-380-1562

● 連絡先 ── 阿含宗に関するご質問・お問い合わせは左記まで

阿含宗本山・釈迦山大菩提寺　京都市山科区北花山大峰町

関東別院　〒108-8318　東京都港区三田四-一四-一五　TEL(〇三)三七六九-一九三一

関西総本部　〒605-0031　京都市東山区三条通り神宮道上ル　TEL(〇七五)七六一-一一四

北海道本部　〒004-0053　札幌市厚別区厚別中央三条三丁目　TEL(〇一一)八九二-九八九一

東北本部　〒984-0051　仙台市若林区新寺一-一三一-一　TEL(〇二二)二九九-五五七一

東海本部　〒460-0017　名古屋市中区松原三-一三-二五　TEL(〇五二)三二四-五五五〇

北陸本部　〒920-0902　金沢市尾張町二-一一-二一　TEL(〇七六)二二四-二六六六

九州本部　〒812-0041　福岡市博多区吉塚五-六-三五　TEL(〇九二)六一一-六九〇一

大阪道場　〒531-0072　大阪市北区豊崎三-八-一〇　TEL(〇六)六三七六-二七二五

神戸道場　〒651-0084　神戸市中央区磯辺通り二-一-一二　TEL(〇七八)二三一-五一五二

広島道場　〒733-0002　広島市西区楠木町一-一三-一-二六　TEL(〇八二)二九三-一六〇〇

横浜道場　〒231-0012　横浜市中区相生町四-七五　JTB・YN馬車道ビル五階・六階　TEL(〇四五)六五〇-二〇五一

沖縄道場　〒900-0031　那覇市若狭一-一〇-九　TEL(〇九八)八六三-八七四三

● インターネットで阿含宗を紹介 ── 阿含宗ホームページ　http://www.agon.org/

●著者紹介

桐山靖雄(きりやま・せいゆう)

阿含宗開祖、中国・国立北京大学名誉教授、中国・国立北京外国語大学名誉教授、中国・国立中山大学名誉教授、中国・国立佛学院(仏教大学)名誉教授、モンゴル国立大学学術名誉教授、名誉哲学博士、モンゴル科学アカデミー名誉哲学博士、チベット仏教ニンマ派仏教大学名誉学長・客員教授、タイ王国・国立タマサート大学ジャーナリズム・マスコミュニケーション学名誉博士、サンフランシスコ大学終身名誉理事、ロンドン大学SOAS名誉フェロー、スリランカ仏教シャム派名誉大僧正、チベット仏教界・ミャンマー仏教界から最高の僧位・法号を授与、ブータン仏教界から法脈相承、秘法皆伝 法号「ンガワン・ゲルツェン(王者の説法をする仏法守護者)」授与、日本棋院名誉九段、中国国際気功研究中心会長(北京)、ダッチ・トゥリートクラブ名誉会員(ニューヨーク)、二〇一六年入滅。

主たる著書『密教・超能力の秘密』『密教・超能力のカリキュラム』『密教占星術Ⅰ・Ⅱ』『説法六十心1・2』『チャンネルをまわせ』『密教誕生』『人間改造の原理と方法』『阿含密教いま』『守護霊を持て』『続・守護霊を持て』『龍神が翔ぶ』『霊障を解く』『一九九九年カルマと霊障からの脱出』『間脳思考』『心のしおり』『愛のために智恵を智恵のために愛を』『末世成仏本尊経講義』『守護霊が持てる冥徳供養』『一九九九年地球壊滅』『守護仏の奇蹟』『求聞持聡明法秘伝』『さあ、やるぞかならず勝つ①~⑫』『仏陀の法』『守護霊と阿含宗』『密教占星術入門』『人は輪廻転生するか』『君は誰れの輪廻転生か』『般若心経瞑想法』『オウム真理教と阿含宗』『阿含仏教・超能力の秘密』『脳と心の革命瞑想』『阿含仏教・超奇蹟の秘密』『一九九七年七月が来る』『社会科学としての阿含仏教』『一九九九年七の月よ、さらば』『21世紀は智慧の時代』(以上)の源流としての阿含仏教』『ニューヨークより世界に向けて発信す』『THE WISDOM OF THE GOMA FIRE CEREMONY』『You Have Been Here Before:Reincarnation』『実践般若心経瞑想法』『変身の原理』『守護神を持て』『止観』『The Marvel of Spiritual Transformation』『輪廻転生瞑想法』『幸福への原理』『仏陀の真実の教えを説く上・中・下』『あなたの人生をナビゲーション』『輪廻転生瞑想法Ⅰ・Ⅱ・Ⅲ』『美しい人になる心のメッセージ』『新装版 輪廻する葦』(以上平河出版社)、『アラディンの魔法のランプ』(阿含宗出版社)、『念力』『超脳思考をめざせ』(徳間書店)、『密教入門──求聞持聡明法の秘密』(角川選書)など。

手を摩擦して眼を覆い、つぎに眼を大きく見開いて、ゆっくりと周囲を見ます。

下肢を按摩して、両脚でしっかりと床を踏みしめて立ち上がります。

ついで座に合掌して去ります。

毎日、一坐はかならず瞑想する習慣をつけることです。

祈りと瞑想。

これによって、ヒトは、カミにもホトケにもなれるのです。

瞑想を終える

瞑想が終わったら、まず、瞑想から心を解き放ちます。

「これで瞑想は終わり。これより自分は、観自在菩薩として、般若の智慧をもって世に立つのである」

と心にはっきりと言い聞かせます。

ムドラーをほどきます。

合掌いたします。

上体をゆっくりと左右に四、五回振りましょう。

つぎに口を開いて、ふーっと気を、三回吐きます。

観自在菩薩大仏光観
かんじざいぼさつだいぶっこうかん

観自在印を組みます。
かんじざいいん

観自在菩薩は、大光明を放ちます。

あなた自身は、観自在菩薩と一体となって大光明を放ちます。

聖 如意光菩薩

印契は如意宝珠印（ムドラー・にょいほうじゅいん）。

大虚空の中に、聖如意光菩薩が現れます。
あなたの般若智は、如意宝珠となります。
如意宝珠は、大光明を放って輝きます。

あなたの印の中に如意宝珠があり、燦然と輝き、虚空中に大光明を放ちます。

三角智印(さんかくちいん)

印契(ムドラー)はアーカーシャ・ムドラー。

前の一大円空の中に、火炎が現れます。

それが三角智印へと変化してゆきます。

あなたの般若智(はんにゃち)は、智印(ちいん)となって炎上します。

智印の大火炎は、大虚空(だいこくう)に遍満(へんまん)いたします。

べ、コトバの円に入れます。

概念は概念の円に入れます。概念がすぐに想い浮かばない場合には、憎しみの心を凝縮して、概念の円に入れます。

あなたのすべての想いと心を、この三つに分類し、おのおのの円に入れましょう。怒りも、怨みも、苦しみも、煩悩すべてを分類して、おのおのの円に入れるのです。自己も円の内に入れましょう。

円の内なるものを一つ一つ消滅させ、それぞれを全くの円空（えんくう）とします。

最後に自分をも消し去り、おなじく円空といたします。

すべてを消し、空とし、一大円空としてください。

三角大円空観（さんかくだいえんくうかん）

両膝の上に、アーカーシャ・ムドラーを組みます。

空間に、巨大な三角形を想い描きます。

それぞれの角に、大きな円をつくります。

自己の想念を、三つに分けます。

形あるものは形像（けいぞう）の円に入れます。具体的な形あるものを思い浮かべてください。もし、思い浮かべるものに迷うならば、あなたが一番、憎しみを感じている人物を思い浮かべ、それを形像の円に入れます。

コトバはコトバの円に入れます。入れるコトバに迷うなら、憎しみのコトバを思い浮か

き、悲しみ、あるいは喜ぶ。しかし、人の性(こころ)の内に、歎き、悲しみ、喜びの、一定の性(しょう)があるわけではない。
因縁因果(いんねんいんが)の理法(りほう)によって、因に応じて縁が動き、かりに相(すがた)をあらわすだけなのだ。これを空(くう)の理(り)と云うのである。

森羅万象、人間関係、その他すべてを、この縁起流転水想観に準じて想念せよ。

（意訳「般若心経」）

縁起流転水想観（えんぎるてんすいそうかん）

舎利子（わがでし）よ。

その教えをここに説こう。

形があっても形にとらわれてはならない。縁あってかりに形を生じたものならば、縁によっては、形なきものに変わる。形がなくとも無しと思ってはならない。縁によっては、形を生じ相（すがた）をあらわす。かの水を見よ。熱する縁をあたえれば熱湯となり、蒸気となって空（そら）にとけこむ。寒冷の縁にあえばかたい氷となり、つめたい霜の柱となる。しかし、水の自性（しょう）に変りなく、ただ縁によって変化するのだ。

世のこと、すべてみな同様だ。形あるも無きも本（もと）は一体にして、すべて因縁次第である。人の心（こころ）の作用（はたらき）の、受も想も行も、識のはたらき、すべてこの理（ことわり）にほかならない。人は歎（なげ）

ぼ（ジャ）字変じて般若波羅蜜多菩薩となる

経台印を組みます。

菩薩の左第一手の梵篋より、大光明が放たれます。

この光明が、あなたの経台印に注がれます。

あなたの経台印は、しだいに光明を放ちます。

以上を観想します。

月輪中に（ジャ）字出現

虚心合掌いたします。

白浄（びゃくじょう）の月輪中に、ジャ字が浮かび出現いたします。

ジャ字は、金色の大光明を放ち輝いております。

ꜱ （娑）字変じて観自在菩薩となる

観自在印を組みます。

この観自在菩薩は、全身より大光明を放ちます。

金色の光明を放って輝いている娑字が変じて、観自在菩薩が出現いたします。

この光明が、あなた自身に照り映えます。

あなたの身も観自在菩薩が放つ光明を受けて、しだいに光を放ち始めます。

あなたの身は全身より光を放ち、観自在菩薩と一体となるのです。

月輪中（がちりんちゅう）に 𐀁（娑（さ））字出現

虚心合掌（こしんがっしょう）いたします。

白浄（びゃくじょう）の月輪中に、娑字がしだいに現れてきます。

その娑字は、金色（こんじき）の光明（こうみょう）を放って輝いています。

月輪観(がちりんかん)

月輪観を修します。

印契(ムドラー)は、アーカーシャ・ムドラー。両膝の上に、アーカーシャ・ムドラーを組んで置きます。

白淨(びゃくじょう)の満月が、眼前二メートルの中空にかかっています。

眼を閉じ、ゆっくりと白淨の月輪を胸中に引き入れます。

その白淨の月輪がしだいに大きくなり、無限大の大きさに拡大します。

無限大の月輪を、しだいにもとの大きさに戻します。

つぎに、眼を開け、月輪を中空に返します。

大虚空観(だいこくうかん)

これから、大虚空観を観想いたします。

印契(ムドラー)は、アーカーシャ・ムドラー。腕を自然に伸ばし、両膝の上に手を置き、親指と人差し指で輪をつくるのがアーカーシャ・ムドラーです。

自分の心に、銀河系・太陽系を越えた遙か彼方の、果てしなき大虚空を想い浮かべます。

その大虚空の中心にわが身を置き、坐します。

般若心経読誦

般若心経を、微音または心読にて読誦いたします。

誓願(せいがん)

誓願いたします。

「謹(つつし)んで、釈迦牟尼世尊(しゃかむにせそん)、ならびに、観自在菩薩摩訶薩(かんじざいぼさつまかさつ)、般若波羅蜜多菩薩摩訶薩(はんにゃはらみたぼさつまかさつ)に申し上げます。

これより私は、観自在菩薩となって、深(じん)般若波羅蜜多の行(ぎょう)に入ります。

なにとぞ御加護(ごかご)によって、無魔行満(むまぎょうまん)いたしますよう、心からお願い申し上げます」

合掌
がっしょう

合掌いたします。

礼拝
らいはい

礼拝いたします。

開経偈
かいきょうげ

開経偈を読誦いたします
どくじゅ

無上甚深微 妙法
むじょうじんじんみ みょうほう

百千万劫難遭遇
ひゃくせんまんごうなんぞうぐう

我今見聞得受持
がこんけんもんとくじゅじ

願解如来真実義
がんげにょらいしんじつぎ

般若心経瞑想法の解説

数息観で最も大切なことは、息と数とを一致させることです。ひたすら「心を数に傾けて、呼吸の行方を心の眼で追うようにして」その心の眼のほうにウエイトを置くようにします。

数息観を適宜行なって、心が安定したところで、つぎに移りましょう。

数息観(すそくかん)

長出入息呼吸法で心が調ったら、数息観に入ります。

文字通り、心を数に集中して、散乱させないための観法です。

これには「出息入息観」「出息観」「入息観」という伝統的な方法があります。

しかし、ここではつぎのようにいたします。

出る息を丹田(たんでん)から天地に向かって吐き出すような気持ちで吐き、その吐いた息の行方を心の眼で追うようにして、声には出さずに、「ヒトー」と数え、ついで息を吐ききってから吸う息で「ツー」と数えます。

こうして十までできたら、またはじめの一に戻って、これを何度もくり返すのです。

大切なことは、吐く息と吸う息の転ずるところが、丸くスムーズに、全体の呼吸が卵形を描く気持ちで行なうことです。具体的には、全部吐ききらないうちに吸い始め、まだいくらか吸えるところで、セーブして吐き始めるようにすると、自然に丸みをおびた楽な呼吸になります。

同時に、必ず鼻からちょっと息を漏らします。これをやらないと、胸から頭部にかけて圧がかかり、身体を痛めるおそれがあります。腹式呼吸をして、頭痛をおこしたり、内臓下垂に苦しむのは、これを知らないからです。

長出息呼吸

つぎに長出息呼吸に移ります。歯は軽くかみ合わせて、かみ合わせた歯の間を通してゆっくりと息を吐きます。下腹に一段と力をこめ、下腹部を収縮させながら、どこまでも腹の力をもって静かに息を吐き出していきます。

長出入息呼吸法

長入息呼吸と長出息呼吸のくり返しが、長出入息呼吸法です。この呼吸法は、一呼吸についての時間は問いません。できるだけ細く、長く、出入息させるのです。

三回から五回くらい、くり返しましょう。

の調った相(すがた)なのです。

呼吸法訓練

呼吸法は、必ず、まず最初に息を吐くことから始めます。歯は軽くかみ合わせて、かみ合わせた歯の間を通して、ゆっくりと息を吐き出します。つぎに吸うときから第一回目の呼吸が始まるのです。

長入息呼吸(ちょうにゅうそくこきゅう)

まず軽く息を吸います。
歯の間を通してゆっくりと息を吐き終わったら、今度は唇を閉じ、歯をきちんと合わせて、舌の先を上の歯茎のやや上部につけます。
そこで、ごく自然にゆっくりと、鼻から息を吸い込んでいきましょう。
息を吸い終わったら、もう一度、かるく息をのみ、みぞおちを充分に落とし、肛門をぐっと閉じ、下腹にウムと力を入れます。

の緊張を解いてください。

頭部、頸部をごく自然に、真っ直ぐ、きちんとした姿勢をとります。額を心持ち前に出し、下あごを少し引くようにして、頭部、頸部の緊張を解きます。同時に、胸を少し引っ込めるようにして、腹部は少し前に出し、両肩の力をぬいて、自然な姿勢をとりましょう。

両眼は半眼(はんがん)にします。かすかに外光を感じる程度にひとすじの隙間を残して、視線を鼻の先に持っていきます。

肛門をきゅっと締め、上へ引き上げるようにします。

つぎに口をやや丸く開き気味にして、下腹の奥から思う存分に息を吐き出します。からだのなかの不浄なものが、吐く息にしたがって、ことごとくまとめて出ていくものと観想します。出つくしたら口を閉じ、鼻から清い気を入れます。

このようにして深い呼吸を三度ほどくりかえしますが、身息(しんそく)が調和すれば、一度でもよろしいでしょう。

重要なのは、緩ならず急ならざること。ゆったりし過ぎず、せわしからず、これが身体

椅子坐

椅子に坐って静坐する場合には、ベルト、衣服をゆるやかに、腰を浅くかけて、両股を少し開き、両足を正しく地につけます。

大和ずわり（正坐）

どうしても、結跏趺坐も半跏趺坐もできない人は、大和ずわり（正坐）にしてください。このときには、膝頭をくっつけないで、両膝頭の間に、男性は拳が三つくらいならんで入るほど、女性は二つならんで入るほど開きます。これで安定します。坐蒲を尻の下に敷くと、坐はさらに安定いたします。

身体を調(ととの)える

まず自分のからだを揉みほぐしてください。
脚を組む前に、足首を回してほぐしします。
つぎに、からだを前や左右に七、八度揺り動かしたり、首や肩を回すなどして、からだ

が自然にできるので、もっともすぐれた坐法といえましょう。左右の脚を、逆に組んでもかまいません。

半跏趺坐（はんかふざ）

結跏趺坐が一番安定したよい坐り方ですが、はじめのうちはなかなか脚が組めないので、半跏趺坐という略式の坐り方でもよろしいでしょう。

右足の土踏まずを、左の内股にピタリとつけて、左足だけを右の腿の上にあげます。足が痛くなったら、足を組みかえてください。

このとき注意しなければならないのは、あげた脚の膝頭が浮かないようにすることです。足が浮いていては不安定で正しい坐法の姿勢にならないので、このときには、尻に敷いている坐蒲をもう一枚重ねて高くしましょう。そうして、少々上体を前に倒して、まず両脚の膝頭をつけ、それからおもむろに上体を真っ直ぐに起こします。

坐の組み方

般若心経瞑想法は、坐っても、椅子に腰掛けて行なってもかまいません。気軽に、リラックスして坐ることが大切です。座所に向かって合掌してから坐ります。

結跏趺坐（けっかふざ）

坐蒲に尻をおろして両方の脚を前にのばし、まず右足の親指のあたりを持って、これを左の腿の上にのせます。このときカカトが下腹につくくらい深くのせましょう。つぎに、左の足指を持って、これもまた右の腿の上に同じように深くのせます。こうして両脚を組み、土踏まずが天井を向くように坐ります。

これが結跏趺坐です。

「カナエの三足」といって、両方の膝頭（ひざがしら）と尾骨の三点がピタリと地について、坐ったからだの底面で二等辺三角形ができるようにすることが大切です。結跏趺坐の場合は、これ

はじめに

まず、静坐（せいざ）、すなわち静かに坐ります。そのために、坐蒲（ざふ）を用意します。坐蒲の代わりに座ぶとんを二つ折りにして用いてもよろしいでしょう。座に着いたら、どっしりと落ち着いて、安楽に坐ります。

合掌

最初に合掌いたします。

香を点ずる

線香は、瞑想の時間を知るためにも、用いたほうがよろしいでしょう。

要は時間の長さより、毎日、一坐はかならず瞑想する習慣をつけることです。はじめは少々苦しくても、しだいに楽しくなり、瞑想せずにはいられなくなるとしめたものです。

瞑想に習熟してくると、DVDを用いずに自分の心の中に映像を思い描いて瞑想を行なえるようになります。そうなるまで瞑想を深めましょう。

瞑想は始めたからといってすぐに何かの効能があるというものではありません。しかし、持続すればかならず驚くような変化がおきるのです。

西洋の古諺にこうあります。

「いまだかつて偉大な仕事をなしとげた人で、瞑想の習慣を持たぬ人はいなかった」

般若心経瞑想法は、「般若心経」にもとづいた瞑想を、誰もが、いつでも、どこでもできるように構成したものです。これを瞑想者が、より明確に習得できるように映像化してDVDにおさめたものが本書です。

そして、般若心経は、「聖者の空の諦り」を体得するためのテキストなのです。あなたも、観自在菩薩となって、般若波羅蜜多の瞑想を行じましょう。

仏陀の時代から、仏教では、真理を知り、煩悩を断じ、そのために修行してきました。

一回の瞑想の長さは（坐してから座を去るまで）、初めは十五分くらいからだんだんにのばして、三十分か四十分くらい瞑想できるようにいたしましょう。

瞑想は、順に行なうのが基本ですが、坐の組み方や呼吸法、観想などを習得できるまで、くりかえし行なってください。また、瞑想を長く行ないたいときは、静止画像を用いてください。

瞑想時の呼吸は、静かなゆっくりとした呼吸で行ないます。

瞑想法入門

印契

「般若根本無尽蔵呪」を誦するときの印契は、経台（きょうだい）印。

この印契、高座（こうざ）（経台）の上に経蔵を安置するようにして、心にあてて、これを着けます。真言を誦するとき、「一切の経蔵みなこの印より出でて、ことごとく心中に入ると観念せよ。無尽蔵の経蔵を出生（しゅっしょう）して、よく一切の般若波羅蜜の法を照了（しょうりょう）す」と想念を集中いたします。

「般若波羅蜜多菩薩印明」を誦するときの印契は、梵篋（ぼんきょう）印。

左の掌（たなごころ）をのべて、右の掌でこれを覆い、左の心（むね）にあてる梵篋（ぼんきょう）印を組んで、この真言を三遍（さんぺん）唱えれば、無量劫（むりょうこう）の愚癡業種（ぐちごうしゅ）を滅して般若波羅蜜円満し、聡明智慧（そうみょうちえ）を獲得するといいます。

この種字は、生不可得(しょうふかとく)、諍論不可得(じょうろんふかとく)の義をあらわします。

真言(こんごん)

般若大心陀羅尼(はんにゃだいしんだらに)
　跢姪他(タニヤタ)　掲帝掲帝(ギャティギャティ)　波羅掲帝(ハラギャティ)
　波羅僧掲帝(ハラソウギャティ)　菩提沙婆訶(ボウジソワカ)

般若根本無尽蔵呪
　那謨婆伽筏帝(ノウボバギャバティ)　鉢囉惹波囉弭多曳(ハラシャハラミタエイ)　唵(オン)
　利伊地伊(リイジイ)　室唎(シリ)　輸嚧陀毘社曳(シュロタビシャエイ)　娑婆訶(ソワカ)

般若波羅蜜多菩薩印明
　唵(オン)　地(ヂ)　室哩輸嚕多尾惹曳(シリシュロタビジャエイ)　娑婆訶(ソワカ)

真言

唵 嚩曰囉達磨 紇哩
オン パ ザ ラ ダ ル マ キリク

印契

印契は、観自在印。
（ムドラー）

左右の手の指を外に出して結び、左右の人差し指の先をあいささえて丸め、蓮華の葉のように左右の親指をならべ立てます。

般若波羅蜜多菩薩
はんにゃ は ら み た ぼさつ

般若波羅蜜多菩薩は、般若の智慧を代表する仏であります。般若の智慧によって悟りを得、仏陀たりうるので、般若波羅蜜多菩薩は仏母といわれるのです。

種字

種字は、 （ジャ）字。

印契とは

印契とは、手と指をさまざまな形につくり、それを組み合わせて、諸仏の悟りを象徴したものです。

観自在菩薩（かんじざいぼさつ）

現実のこの世界において、四苦八苦に苦しむ衆生を救済することが、仏教の実践です。その代表が、三十三身に変化して、衆生の厄難を救い、福徳を与える観自在菩薩であります。

種子

観自在菩薩の種字は、**ऄ**（娑（さ））字。

三諦不可得（さんたいふかとく）の義（ぎ）で、有・空（くう）・中の三諦（さんたい）をもって、迷いの中にいる一切衆生（いっさいしゅじょう）を悟りに目覚めさせることを表しています。

以上は原則で、いつ、どこでも、どんな状態でも瞑想に入れるよう心がけてください。そして自由に、気楽に、のびのびと瞑想してください。

種字（しゅじ）・真言（マントラ）・印契（ムドラー）

般若心経瞑想法のなかで用いる、種字・真言・印契を説明いたします。

種字とは

種字とは、梵字（ぼんじ）の一字を以て、仏・菩薩などがそなえている力を表したものです。草木の種子（たね）が雨・露・日光などの縁を得て、根・茎・葉・花などを生じるように、一字に仏・菩薩の諸功徳が含まれていることから、種字といいます。

真言とは

真言とは、仏・菩薩などの誓いや徳、諦（さと）りや教えの深い意味がこもった真実の言葉を指します。

食べものは、栄養をよく考えて、バランスのとれた食事を摂りましょう。食べものの摂り方で、人間は心の状態、脳のはたらきなどがかわるものです。

つぎに、睡眠不足もよくありませんが、眠ることが必要度を越えて多いときは、かえって心を弛緩(しかん)させるので、適度に調節しましょう。

また、瞑想する人は、つねに、息を細く長く、乱れないように心がけてください。息づかいが荒いと、心も乱れて、おさめにくくなります。

瞑想する、しないにかかわらず、人間はつねに呼吸を調(ととの)えなければいけません。動作が粗雑であると、息づかいが乱れます。息づかいが乱れると、思考も粗雑になるのです。呼吸が調っている人は、心も安定しているのです。その反対に、心を安定させたければ、息を調え、安定させることです。

衣服は、厚着にもならず、薄着にもならず、寒からず暑からずの服装で、清潔なものがよいでしょう。帯、ベルトなどをゆるやかにして、意識がひっかからないようにしてください。

瞑想の準備

それでは、これから瞑想に入る前の準備を説明いたしましょう。

瞑想するには、特別な仕度はいりません。

瞑想の場所は、なるべく気の散らない静かな場所がよろしいでしょう。

あまり大きな部屋では集中しにくく、小さすぎる部屋は気がこもってくるので、六畳ぐらいの部屋がよいでしょう。

部屋は清潔にして、明るすぎたり、暗すぎない状態にします。また、寒くもなく、暑すぎないよう調節してください。

正面にマンダラをかけ、香華(こうげ)、すなわち線香と花を供えます。

線香は、瞑想の時間を知るためのものでもあります。用いたほうがよいでしょう。

ものを食べて直ぐ、満腹の状態、あるいは逆に、あまりに空腹のときは避けたほうがよいでしょう。

般若心経瞑想法とは

この般若心経を、だれでも容易に瞑想できるよう具体的に構成したのが「般若心経瞑想法」です。

「空の諦（さと）り」を体得するには、般若心経を何千回、何万回読誦しても、到達できません。般若心経マンダラによる「聖者の瞑想」によってのみ、それは可能となるのです。

修行者はまず観自在（かんじざい）の定（じょう）に入って、深般若波羅蜜多（じんはんにゃはらみった）の瞑想を行（ぎょう）じるのです。すなわち、あなた自身が、観自在菩薩（かんじざいぼさつ）となって般若波羅蜜多の行をなし、智慧を身につけるのです。

歩めよ、歩めよ、ただ歩めよ、歩めばやがて行きつかんすべてを解脱（げだつ）した彼の岸（か）に。スヴァーハー。

般若心経とは

仏教の経典は、約七千余巻といわれています。そのなかで、もっとも短く、二六二字にて仏教の心髄を簡潔に説いているのが、「般若心経」です。このお経は、功徳の大きいお経といわれ、日本だけでなく、広くアジア各地でも読誦されております。

「般若波羅蜜多心経」を訳すと、「最高の智慧の行の極限において、彼岸に到達した中心眼目の経」となります。ニルヴァーナ（解脱）は仏陀の教えの究極の目標であり、智慧の行はその目標に到達するための手段、方法なのです。

つまり、般若心経は仏陀の原点である「智慧の行」に戻ることを説く経典であり、「聖者の空の諦り」を体得するための瞑想のテキストなのです。

般若心経瞑想法への誘い

たあることなし。また、眼に見るところもなく、意識界もなし、以て意識界もなし、従って無明の尽くるところもなく、迷いの尽くるところも、苦も、集も、滅も、道も智慧もなく、所得もなしと悟れ。一切心にとどむべからず、これを悟らば一切の罣礙心より去るべし。心に罣礙なければ、迷いも恐れも欲も生ぜず、菩提薩埵はすべからく此の空の真理を体現すべし。顛倒を離れてかならず涅槃を究竟つくさん。

三世に住みたまえる一切の御仏は、このさとりによって因縁解脱を成就し給えり。この故に、解脱を求めんとする人は、すべからく、般若波羅蜜多の大神呪を知らねばならぬ。この大神呪は無上の呪文にして、無比の呪文なり。いっさいの苦厄災難を解脱る呪文にして、その威力はかり難し、すべての真理の中の真理と云うべし。真理であるが故に、いつの世よ、いかなる時においても変らず、虚偽あやまりならず。

その呪に説いて曰く、
「空の真理を身につけて、観自在の慈悲のもと、行ぜよ、行ぜよ、ただひたすらに。因縁解脱の彼の岸にあゆめばやがて行き着かん。

なる。水の自性に変りなく、ただ縁によってかく変化す。世のことすべてみなこの如し、形あるも無きも本は一体にして、すべて因縁次第なり。人の心の作用の、受も想も行も、識のはたらき、すべてこの理にほかならず。人は歎き、悲しみ、あるいは喜ぶ、されど、人の性の内に、歎き、悲しみ、喜びの、一定の性のあるにはあらず。り、因に応じ、縁が動いて、かりに相をあらわすのみ。これを空の理と云うぞ。舎利子よ。

このように、諸法の大本は、空なる相である故に、現象の上に於ては縁によって様々に変化をあらわすけれども、その本体はいささかも変ることなし。生ずることもなければ、滅することもなく、垢るることもなければ、浄まるということもなし。減ることもなければ、増すこともなし。ただあるものは変化のみ。

この道理を悟って、この世の成立を見るならば、色あるものも形なきにひとしく、受も、想も、行も、識のはたらきすべて有ることなし。また、それらの本なる眼も耳も鼻も舌も身も意もあるにあらず。また、六根の対象たる色も声も香りも味わいも触も法もま

意訳　般若心経

聖なる観自在菩薩は、世のひとすべての悩みを救う真理を求めて、いとふかき般若の行に入り給えり。

この行の波羅蜜多において、聖なる観自在菩薩は、この世のものすべて、五蘊いっさいは、本来空なるものと照見たまいて、この真理をもって、世のひとすべての悩み苦しみを解きほどく真実の道となし給えり。

舎利子よ。

その教えをここに説くならば、形ありとて形にとらわるべからず。縁あってかりに形を生じたものなれば、縁によっては、また、形なき空なるものに変らん。また、形なしとて無しと思うな、縁によっては、形を生じ相をあらわす。たとえば、かの水を見よ。熱するという縁をあたうれば熱湯となり、蒸気となって空にとけこむ。さむればふたたび水となり、雨となって地に降りそそぐ。寒冷の縁にあわばかたき氷となり、つめたき霜の柱と

乃至、老死も無く、また老死の尽くることも無し。
苦も集も滅も道も無く、智も無く、また得も無し。
所得無きを以ての故に。
菩提薩埵は、般若波羅蜜多に依るが故に、心に罣礙無し。
罣礙無きが故に、恐怖あること無く、
一切の顛倒夢想を遠離し、
涅槃を究竟す。三世の諸仏も般若波羅蜜多に依るが故に、
阿耨多羅三藐三菩提を得たまえり。
故に知るべし、般若波羅蜜多は是れ大神呪なり。
是れ大明呪なり、是れ無上呪なり、是れ無等等呪なり。
よく一切の苦を除く。真実にして虚しからざるが故に。
般若波羅蜜多の呪を説く。すなわち呪を説いて曰く、
掲帝、掲帝、般羅掲帝、般羅僧掲帝、菩提僧莎訶
般若（波羅蜜多）心経。

般羅僧掲帝（はーらーそうぎゃーてい）。
菩提僧莎訶（ぼーじーそーわーかー）。
般若（波羅蜜多）心経（はんにゃはらみったしんぎょう）。

観自在菩薩。深般若波羅蜜多を行ずる時、五蘊皆空なりと照見して、一切の苦厄を度したもう。
舎利子よ。色は空に異ならず、空は色に異ならず。色は即ち是れ空、空は即ち是れ色なり。受・想・行・識もまたかくの如し。
舎利子よ。是の諸法は空相にして、生ぜず、滅せず、垢（け）れず、浄（きよ）からず、増すこと無く、減ること無し。
是の故に、空の中には色も無く、受・想・行・識も無し。
眼・耳・鼻・舌・身・意も無く、色・声・香・味・触・法も無し。眼界も無く、乃至、意識界も無し。
無明も無く、また無明の尽くることも無し。

依般若波羅蜜多故（えーはんにゃはーらーみったーこー）。
得阿耨多羅三藐三菩提（とくあーのくたーらーさんみゃくさんぼーだい）。
故知般若波羅蜜多（こーちーはんにゃはーらーみったー）。
是大神呪（ぜーだいじんしゅ）。
是大明呪（ぜーだいみょうしゅ）。
是無上呪（ぜーむーじょうしゅ）。
是無等等呪（ぜーむーとうどうしゅ）。
能除一切苦（のうじょいっさいくー）。
真実不虚故（しんじつふーこーこー）。
説般若波羅蜜多呪（せつはんにゃはーらーみったーしゅ）。
即説呪曰（そくせつしゅわつ）
掲帝（ぎゃーてい）。
掲帝（ぎゃーてい）。
般羅掲帝（はーらーぎゃーてい）。

亦無無明尽（やくむーむーみょうじん）。
乃至無老死（ないしーむーろうしー）。
亦無老死尽（やくむーろうしーじん）。
無苦集滅道（むーくーじゅうめつどう）。
無智亦無得（むーちーやくむーとく）。
以無所得故（いーむーしょとくこー）。
菩提薩埵（ぼーだいさったー）。
依般若波羅蜜多故（えーはんにゃはーらーみったーこー）。
心無罣礙（しんむーけーげー）。
無罣礙故（むーけーげーこー）。
無有恐怖（むーうーくーふー）。
遠離〔一切〕顛倒夢想（おんりーいっさいてんどうむーそー）。
究竟涅槃（くーぎょうねーはん）。
三世諸仏（さんぜーしょぶつ）。

受想行識亦復如是（じゅそうぎょうしきやくぶーにょぜー）。

舎利子（しゃーりーしー）。

是諸法空相（ぜーしょほうくうそう）。

不生不滅（ふーしょうふーめつ）。

不垢不浄（ふーくーふーじょう）。

不増不減（ふーぞうふーげん）。

是故空中（ぜーこーくうちゅう）。

無色（むーしき）。

無受想行識（むーじゅそうぎょうしき）。

無眼耳鼻舌身意（むーげんにーびーぜっしんにー）。

無色声香味触法（むーしきしょうこうみーそくほう）。

無眼界（むーげんかい）。

乃至無意識界（ないしーむーいーしきかい）。

無無明（むーむーみょう）。

仏説摩訶般若波羅蜜多心経

唐三蔵法師玄奘＝訳

観自在菩薩（かんじーざいぼーさー）。
行深般若波羅蜜多時（ぎょうじんはんにゃはーらーみったーじー）。
照見五蘊皆空（しょうけんごーうんかいくう）。
度一切苦厄（どーいっさいくーやく）。
舎利子（しゃーりーしー）。
色不異空（しきふーいーくう）。
空不異色（くうふーいーしき）。
色即是空（しきそくぜーくう）。
空即是色（くうそくぜーしき）。

般若心経読誦

- 開経偈 …… 42
- 般若心経読誦 …… 43
- 誓願 …… 43
- 大虚空観 …… 44
- 月輪観 …… 45
- 月輪中に 𑖾 (娑さ) 字出現 …… 46
- 月輪中に 𑖾 (娑さ) 字変じて観自在菩薩となる …… 47
- 月輪中に 𑖕 (ジャ) 字出現 …… 48
- 月輪中に 𑖕 (ジャ) 字変じて般若波羅蜜多菩薩となる …… 49
- 縁起流転水想観 …… 50
- 三角大円空観 …… 52
- 三角智印 …… 54
- 聖如意光菩薩 …… 55
- 観自在菩薩大仏光観 …… 56
- 瞑想を終える …… 57

結跏趺坐	33
半跏趺坐	34
椅子坐	35
大和ずわり（正坐）	35
身体を調える	35
呼吸法訓練	37
長入息呼吸	37
長出息呼吸	38
長出入息呼吸法	38
数息観	39

般若心経瞑想法の解説 …… 41

合掌	42
礼拝	42

観自在菩薩 …… 25
　種字 …… 25
　真言 …… 26
　印契 …… 26
般若波羅蜜多菩薩 …… 26
　種字 …… 26
　真言 …… 27
　印契 …… 28

瞑想法入門 …… 29

はじめに …… 32
合掌 …… 32
香を点ずる …… 32
坐の組み方 …… 33

般若心経読誦 … 9

仏説摩訶般若波羅蜜多心経 … 10

意訳 般若心経 … 16

般若心経瞑想法への誘い … 19

般若心経とは … 20

般若心経瞑想法とは … 21

瞑想の準備 … 22

種字・真言・印契 … 24

種字とは … 24

真言とは … 24

印契とは … 25

実践般若心経瞑想法　目次

普及版 実践 般若心経瞑想法

2002年1月25日　第1版第1刷発行
2019年2月1日　普及版第1版第1刷発行

著者　桐山靖雄
©2002 by Seiyu KIRIYAMA
発行者——和田尚子
発行所——株式会社 平河出版社
〒108-0073 東京都港区三田 3-4-8
電話 03(3454)4885 FAX.03(5484)1660
郵便振替 00110-4-117324

装幀——佐藤篤司
印刷所——凸版印刷 株式会社
用紙店——中庄 株式会社

落丁・乱丁本はお取り替えいたします。
Printed in Japan
ISBN978-4-89203-350-6 C0015
本書の引用は自由ですが、必ず出版社の承諾を得ること。

実践般若心経瞑想法

桐山靖雄

平河出版社

桐山靖雄・阿含宗開祖